THERE IS A
LIGHT ON
IN ADDICT
THE
IN

JOHN VINSON

authorHOUSE®

AuthorHouse™
1663 Liberty Drive
Bloomington, IN 47403
www.authorhouse.com
Phone: 1 (800) 839-8640

Published by AuthorHouse 07/26/2019

ISBN: 978-1-7283-2074-8 (sc)
ISBN: 978-1-7283-2072-4 (hc)
ISBN: 978-1-7283-2073-1 (e)

Library of Congress Control Number: 2019910484

ACKNOWLEDGMENTS

Many are the times that God has brought me through. If I would speak or write of them, they would be too numerous to count. There is none to compare to Him.

To my five children, Joan, Elesta, John II, Maxine and my late daughter Jennessia. To my grand children, Jennessia H, Tawana, Brittany, Delcina, Derick Jr, Curtis Jr, John lll, Jayci and five great grand- children and a host of step children. My children are the sunshine of my life and evidence that God restores Families.

To my late father, John T. Vinson. My late Mother, Roxie Farr, Vinson, Price, whom we miss so very much. To my brothers, Mac Arthur, Jeremiah, George. My sisters, Ernestine, Maxine, Delcine, Lena and my late sister Naomi.

Minister John L. Vinson I

President/Founder. Teen Outreach Academy

CONTENTS

WHAT THIS BOOK CONTAINS

Mysteries of God and Wise Men of Yesterday

Jesus said that even the prophets and righteous men of the Old Testament desire to see and hear what's in these parables.

Secrets

Over a hundred of them.

Bullet Points

This book is designed for clarity, not confusion. A bullet point is not necessarily a sentence. The layout takes you straight to the point, intentionally leaving out reason and assuming and allowing you to identify key issues and facts quickly.

Stories

True stories from my life experiences and others with good morals to live by.

Pyramid Diagram: Character Quality/Character Defect

This book will give you a clear understanding of the importance of character; your character determines your successes and failures.

This book contains a pyramid demonstrating how bad character brings about ugliness and causes you to search outside of yourself for joy, peace, and happiness only to find short-term pleasure leading to long-term pain.

Good character brings you joy, peace, and happiness. The good feeling you have for yourself encourages you and gives you confidence that you will value more than destructive behavior. This positive good character allows for you to say no to destructive behaviors that can lead to addictions.

Do you want to get well? Do you want help? Do you want change? In this book, you will learn why we fall off our wagons. Right from the beginning, God gave us the ability to experience inner joy, peace, and happiness.

When we turn away from God, our Creator, we turn to the enemy, our destroyer.

Our inner selves will never be happy if our souls are miserable. When our souls are miserable, we'll turn to addictions.

Solomon, the wisest man ever, wrote of alcoholism and its consequences. What he wrote applies also to eating disorders and addictions to illegal drugs, pornography, gambling, adultery, and so on.

> Who has woe? Who has sorrow? Who has strife? Who has complaints? Who has needless bruises? Who has bloodshot eyes? Those who linger over wine, who goes to sample bowls of mixed wine's Do not gaze at wine when it is red, when it sparkles in the cup, when it goes down smoothly! In the end it bites like a snake and poisons like a viper. Your eyes will see strange sights and your mind imagine confusing things. You will be like one sleeping on the high seas, lying on top of the rigging. "They hit me," you will say, "but I'm not hurt! They beat me, but I don't feel it! When will I wake up so I can find another drink?" (Proverbs 23:29–35)

Visual Diagram of High Love and Low Love

This is a good source of information for parents, teachers, caregivers, counselors, and others that includes tips on how to use skills to communicate effectively by responding to your loved ones and others in your care with dysfunctional behaviors.

Parables of Light

> In him was life; and the life was the light of men. And the light shineth in darkness; and the darkness comprehended it not. (John 1:4–5)

This book is filled with many biblical parables and others written by everyday wise men and women.

After Jesus had finished speaking to a crowd of people, the disciples asked Jesus, "Why do you speak to the people in parables?" Jesus said to the disciples, "In these times and days the heart of man has grown dull. I speak in parables that the people may know the mysteries of God. With their ear the people scarcely hear and they have closed their eyes." Jesus said, "God can and will heal you if you turn to see, to hear, and to understand with your hearts." He told the disciples that even the prophets and righteous men of the Old Testament desired to see and hear what was in his parables.

Jesus is now passing it down to you.

I will open my mouth in parables. I will utter things hidden since the creation of the world.

Question

The thing I said I'm going to do, I find myself not doing it. The thing I said I'm not going to do, I find myself doing the very thing I hate. If I'm doing the very thing I hate, is it me who is doing it?

Answer

Now I understand my past behavior. A problem is a problem is a problem. Some problems will spiral you downward faster than others.

Secret: You want to know whether you are suffering from an addiction? What is the first thing that comes to mind when you are alone?

Eating Disorders

Food should be portioned just as a pharmacy measures a medication—just enough. Do you live to eat, or do you eat to live? Man is ruled by his appetite. Man shall not live by bread alone. Esau sold his birthright for a bowl of soup (Genesis 25:33). It is not what you eat; it's what's eating you. Doctors have determined that all diseases start in the stomach—the gut.

Secret: When you are eating, the moment you feel you have had enough, stop! Wrap it up for a later time; you'll have turned one meal into two.

Drug Addictions

Addictions are good only when you're indulging in them. You end up worse off than before. For a while, you'll think you have it, but it won't be long before it will have you. Short-term pleasure ends up being long-term pain.

Alcoholism

Give strong drink to him that is ready to perish. (Proverbs 31:6)

Pornography

The Bible says it is better to put seed in the belly of a whore than to put it on the ground. Pornography promotes incompetency and shame. Sometimes, we can't enjoy God's gift of fulfillment because we have turned to artificial intelligence and have fallen in love with self. Our seed is sacred; everything to make human life is in our seed.

Gambling

Vegas was built on the backs of losers. Money promises you everything God does, but you can't serve God and Mammon.

Can God trust you enough to bless you?

Adultery

Adultery comes from the word *idol*. Sex is a God-given desire to strengthen the relationship between husband and wife. God wants us to understand the difference between lust and love. One reason some marriages don't last is that they were built on lust, not love.

When you are cheating in your marriage, you are stealing.

How to Use This Book

Each bullet point stands on its own. The phrase or sentence before or after each bullet point may be a companion to the point. These old sayings and quotes are true. They are ways and means to all things considered.

How bad do you want it? Turn the Light On and look inside of you. If you only see with your eyes, you want see. When you change how you see things, then the things you look at began to change. You can't find peace until you find all the pieces. This book is design to help save lives. This book can be used as a work book in Group Homes, Shelters, Caregivers, Counselors, Parents or anyone in your care or concern. As Jesus said to the Disciples, "In these days and times the people don't want to hear or see what's in these parables. Give this book as a gift to yourself, love ones or others. You can let the parables, poetry and quotes of this book speak for itself. Jesus explained that this method can be most effective.

Read this book frequently; it's short and easy. You'll start changing without even trying.

INTRODUCTION

"Let there be light" were God's first words. In the beginning was darkness. God created light out of darkness. Creating light was God's work.

Secret: You never know God until you know darkness.

> We are no longer slaves, for the slave knows not what the Master is doing. Jesus said we are his friends and he has made known to us everything he learned from The Father. (John 15:15)

We are God's children. God created us in his image.

This book is about choices and repercussions. Which one are you going to serve—the creature or your Creator?

God has given you a brilliant mind. Use it!

I've spent more than twenty years writing this book. I started in the wilderness. My first job was as a group home staffer in a far-out town where there were mostly cotton fields and prisons.

The words on these pages are written for you and you only. Take every word and every chapter personally. While reading, take an inventory of yourself.

One great man said, "An unexamined life is not worth living."

Use the knowledge of this book to make yourself brilliant.

I am a reaper. Glean behind the reaper. I have already paid the price, paved the way, and made a trail for you to follow.

As you read this book, the light will become brighter. As you begin recognizing the areas of your life that need work, you will be able to let God shape and mold you into a beautiful person everyone will notice. Many lives will be changed because of the change that will take place in your life.

Stop trying to figure it out! You can't. Just read the book. Let the Word do its job. The Word is going to do the changing. Creating light is God's work. You read God's mind when you read his Word. When you get into the Word, the Word will get into you. According to John 1:1,

God and the Word are the same. You are communing with God when you are reading His Word. Allow yourself to become more Christlike.

What you feed your mind determines your appetite—for food, sex, drugs, alcohol, pornography, gambling, and so on.

I gathered many notes to write this book; I wrote them on scraps of paper, napkins, bags, greeting cards, paper plates, and envelopes. I wanted to preserve interesting quotes and powerful proverbs that inspired and strengthened me during my journey from addiction to freedom. I am freely passing all of them on to you.

> No one lights a lamp and puts it in a place where it would be hidden or under a bowl. Instead he puts it on its stand, so that those who come in may see the light. (Luke 11:33)

- Everything God has for you comes in the form of a problem. When you can't solve the problem, that means you're looking in the wrong places for the solution.
- God allows you to go through problems so you can see what's in you.

Secret: How you respond in the problem determines how long you'll have the problem. Not knowing how to turn to God, you turn to the flesh. If you trust in the flesh, you could turn to addictions. When you turn from God's prohibitions, you turn to the enemy.

Secret: Anything you feed the flesh turns to waste.

You were born to fulfill life's promises. Put the problem where the promise is.

God says his way is better and easier. It is not without trials, tribulations, and adversities, but it will be a life full of joy, peace, and happiness.

Be imitators of God as beloved children. (Ephesians 5:1)

Secret: Sin starts with dissatisfaction of where you are now. Feeling ugly on the inside results in no joy, peace, or happiness. This causes you to search outside for a better feeling. Short-term pleasure brings long-term pain. The devil is a trickster. He will try to make wrong look right.

True Story

Once after I had been out using drugs, I got home and went straight to the mirror. I told myself, "Look at you. You haven't combed your hair, you need a shave, and you need new clothes. You need to start doing something for yourself!"

Then it came to me. The Holy Spirit told me, *All you have been doing was for yourself. All that money you spent out there—who was that for? That was for you!*

My eyes began to tear up. A light turned on in my head. Brokenness had begun to take place.

The devil tells you everything except how you're going to end up.

1

CHAPTER

Character

The word *character* means to etch, build, or design into a whole.

Change your character, and you'll live forever.

Our prayer should be this: "God, allow me to see myself the way I really am—not the way I see me but the way you see me, Lord."

James Gordon, a great scholar, wrote about the moral philosophy of character building. He offered four great tests of character.

First is the home test—how someone treats those with whom he or she lives.

Second is the business test—how someone conducts himself or herself with customers and employees.

Third is the social test—how someone acts toward those who do not enjoy the same social advantages as he or she does.

Fourth is the success test—how someone behaves in circumstances that bring him or her wealth, power, position, and honor.

- Sometimes, opening our eyes may show us the most painful thing we've ever encountered.
- The truth hurts. You can be in darkness for so long that it hurts when the light comes on.
- One day, your life will flash before your eyes, so make sure it's worth watching.
- A man is who his character is. A man without a good character becomes a real character.
- Difficult situations define our character. We were born to fulfill life's promises.
- You can't solve a problem until you focus on its cause. You can conquer, but you need to know the whys, what's, and how's of the problem.

Only when you begin to recognize the areas of your life that need work can you begin to let God shape you into a beautiful person everyone will notice. You will influence many lives by the way change will be taking place in your life.

Identify whatever makes you upset, and decide to do something about it. It's time to start turning your pain into power. Yes, you can. Choose life that you might live forever.

- The body can't be happy if the soul is miserable.
- The more peace you have, the more you will enjoy life.
- You can't find peace until you find all the pieces.

Secret: Your outcome can be traced back to your response. You can react to what the devil says or respond to what God says. You can't be saved by what you do by yourself. You can be saved only by what Jesus did on the cross for you. Regardless of what you do, it won't be enough.

We all have parts of our lives we depend on. God targets those areas of our lives for brokenness which ensures our reliance on him and him only to ensure our obedience.

- God is trying to reproduce himself in you. God came into you to reunite with your spirit.
- You were born to live a fulfilled life.
- Jesus is here to break the spirit of addiction.
- You were born to serve others. Jesus was a servant. We are ambassadors of Christ. We are here to be used by God to help win souls for the kingdom of heaven (1 Corinthians 4:16). Be an imitator of Christ.

God made everything for a purpose.

- Unless you know the purpose of something, you will abuse it.
- One of the greatest tragedies is living without purpose.

How do you find purpose? You don't. God will let you know your purpose, but first, you have to be in a position to receive it.

- Purpose means the original intent.

Purpose attracts provisions.

Jesus said that we are his friends and that he is passing on to us everything he learned from the Father.

There are secrets in life. The reason we are defeated is that we are looking in the wrong places for victory. In the natural, things don't make sense.

- You can't hurt yourself without hurting someone else.

Our conduct and character can be so emotionally painful and dysfunctional that we will do anything to kill the pain we feel.

At the Teen Outreach Academy, I worked with teenagers who were called cutters. They were suffering emotionally from such severe pain and hurt usually due to having experienced rejection. They felt that no one loved them. They felt so abandoned and lonely that they would cut themselves, usually on their arms, and actually say that doing so felt good. I even heard that cutting felt like an extreme orgasm. All indications were that cutting was a way they dealt with the emotional pain they felt; that's referred to as transferring pain.

These were teens who had not turned to substance abuse. Those of us who suffer from eating disorders, alcohol abuse, and addictions to pornography, adultery, gambling, drugs, and so on are types of cutters also when we turn to such behaviors to transfer our pain.

But God didn't create us to live lives of constant dissatisfaction.

Secret: How you respond to a problem determines how long you'll have the problem.

The only way God can help you is by putting people and circumstances in your path to purge you of your character defects.

- What looks like a problem could very well be an opportunity. (That's something my father, John T. Vinson, told me.)

Remember that God's vision is to reproduce himself in us. Every child should look like his or her father in terms of character, image, conduct, and more.

God is trying to restore us to his original intent. He wants to fix us and give us back what we have lost. When we listen to the Word of God, we're listening to his thoughts.

Secret: God is more interested in changing you than changing your circumstances.

You don't break God's laws. God's laws break's you. God is the one who catches the wise in their craftiness.

Sin starts with dissatisfaction of where you are now. Sin is an illusion; it's all about *FEAR*—False Evidence Appearing Real. Once sin is full blown, you'll find yourself in Egypt, which represents death. Your spirit will begin to die, and you will find yourself in the slavery of addiction.

Jesus said we are no longer slaves. He is showing us the way out of slavery.

- When God calls us, he is asking us to come and die. When we are living according to the flesh, we must die (Roman 8:13).

Secret: The reason you can't stop the behavior is that you're still alive.

- Your old man, your old nature, has no place in your new life.

God put a Christlike character in us so we would experience joy, peace, and happiness. The Bible tells us we have to be born again. We can't save ourselves, but God can. He allows us to go through situations so he can demonstrate his power to us.

Secret: Other people's lives are changed by our testimony.

If people's character becomes corrupted with defects that they do not recognize and attend to, their souls will become ugly. They will seek joy, peace, and happiness in things that will enslave them including eating disorders, illegal drugs, alcohol, pornography, gambling, adultery, and other addictions. Their good character qualities are below the surface and rarely seen; the ugliness of their character is the only thing others can see.

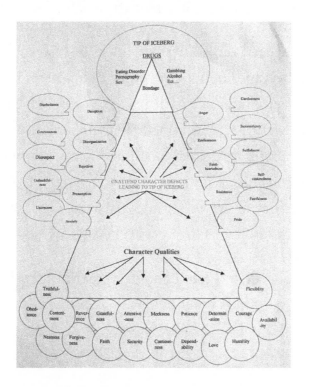

Positive **Character Traits**

Truthfulness

Truthfulness is the first sign of recovery.

Until you're willing to fall flat on your face with honesty, you won't be able to resolve your problems. He who covers his sins shall not prosper.

Sooner or later, God will allow your covers to be pulled off and expose you because he loves you so much that he can't keep his eyes off you.

- Denial is the enemy of truthfulness.
- Happiness must have truthfulness as its foundation.

It hurts when your soul is corrupted by character defects. Your soul becomes ugly to the point that you no longer love yourself. Your inner self will become crippled, paralyzed, hopeless, fearful, and ashamed (Romans 6:21).

God made us to experience peace, joy, happiness, and confidence in him. Life is not without trials, tribulations, and adversities, but we should trust in God more than ourselves and believe God is who he says he is.

- A good lie has just enough element of truth about it that it sounds convincing.

Forgiveness

A the level you understand forgiveness is at the level you will feel forgiven.

- An old African proverb says that he who forgives first ends the quarrel.

- You can't love yourself until you forgive yourself.
- When you don't forgive someone, you are chained to that person.

Secret: Unforgiveness is like eating rat poison and waiting for the rat to die.

Those who try to hurt you are reflections of their pain, not you.

We are all responsible for ourselves.

Regardless of how someone may have offended you, it is your responsibility and choice of <u>responding</u> or reacting.

- Will you respond according to God's Word or react to your offender? Only you are responsible for how you respond.

Forgiveness says, "If I put my hand on it. God takes his hands off of it. If I take my hands off of it, God put's his hands on it."

- Forgiveness unlocks the door to your blessing.

Jesus learned obedience through the things he suffered (Hebrews 5:8). During his journey on earth, he noticed that everything the Father told him was going to happen did happen. That encouraged Jesus to endure until the end.

Hebrews 5:9 says, "Jesus was made perfect because of his endurance."

Secret: We call the valley the low place. God calls the valley the high place. It is in the valley that we grow through trials, tribulations, and adversities.

When we turn away from God we turn to the enemy.

Proverbs 12:15 describes independence from God. When we turn away from God, we end up in the arms of the devil and start down the path to addictions that lead to spiritual and physical death.

According to Romans 2:6, God will render to us according to our deeds.

Jesus is our role model. He knew that as long as he followed the Word, it would lead to the promise. We too should follow the word to victory through faith.

Contentment

One of the best ways to fight off anxiety and depression is to look back and see where God has brought us from.

We should say, "Thank you, Lord, for not giving me what I deserve."

Sin usually starts with being dissatisfied with where we are presently.

We all have our seasons in life—times to cultivate and times to harvest.

The devil will tell you to look at others especially when they are in their season of harvest, and that can cause you to be covetous. The Bible tells us not to be jealous of our neighbors' possessions. If we are envious in that way, we will think, *They have, but I don't. They must be blessed, and I'm not.*

Secret: The Bible says we should esteem others above ourselves. We should look not at things seen but at things unseen.

True Story

One night, I was out late night doing drugs. On my way home in my Corvette, I ran out of gas. I had less than $2. I pulled over and walked about a mile to a gas station and bought what gas I could. I walked back to my car, put the gas in, and drove off.

At a stoplight, a young man pulled up next to me, rolled down his window, and said, "I wish I were in your shoes." I smiled and gave him a thumbs-up, but I thought, *Oh boy, if you only knew!* I'd spent most of the money I had been paid that week on drugs. I was a single parent who had to face my children. I knew they were up worrying about me and wondering if I'd come home with any money. I felt like dirt. I was depressed and hopeless. I wanted to tell that young man, *Mister, if you only knew. What you see might not be what you see.*

Gratefulness

When someone gives you a gift that you think has little value, don't condemn it. Rather, celebrate his or her giving it to you.

True Story

One Christmas, my fiancée gave me only a belt, and I asked, "Is this all you bought me for Christmas?"

But that belt lasted me for three years. I wore it every day. From time to time, she'd ask me, "Now how's that belt?" That taught me to appreciate everyone's gifts. After all, it was a reversible belt—just what I needed.

Be grateful for what you receive; the giver will be grateful for that. Being ungrateful causes stress, depression, and anxiety that if unchecked will allow ugliness to set in.

What God makes starts with nothing and ends up with everything.

- Whoever would have thought that Adam was pregnant with Eve? In a rib was everything needed to make a woman.

Humility

- Everything in the kingdom of God is upside down from what we think it should be.
- We should trust more in God than in ourselves.

The sun, moon, and stars allow us to see the natural world, but God's supernatural Word allows us to walk through darkness.

> The sun shall be no more thou light by day. Neither, for brightness shall the moon give light unto thou, but the Lord shall be unto thou everlasting light and thou God the Glory. (Isaiah 60:19)

The Bible tells us to never think more highly of ourselves that we ought to.

Story

One community voted to give a fellow citizen a medal for being humble. The next day, they took it away because he was wearing it around his neck.

> Do not be overcome by evil, but overcome evil with good. (Romans 12:21)

Never take revenge; leave room for the wrath of God. He said, "Vengeance is mine. I will repay."

Secret: The meek shall inherit the earth.

Secret: If you want to be important, be a servant.

Secret: When you lift others up, they will give back to you.

Secret: God is opposed of the proud, but he gives grace to the humble.

Secret: He who humbles himself shall be exalted.

- Pride is the original sin. Pride means self, me, I, my.
- Pride makes you independent from God (Romans 8:7).
- Pride is an enemy of God. The prideful haven't gotten away with anything; they've just gotten by for the time being.
- Always be humble.
- Count your blessings whenever you're anxious, depressed, restless, or hopeless. Think about how far God has brought you and through what.

Secret: Contemplating God's goodness leads to joy, peace, happiness, and confidence.

Secret: God's kindness leads you to repentance (Romans 2:4).

Love

To love—that is the greatest Commandment. Love God with all your heart, soul, and mind, and love your neighbors as you love yourself.

When we were helpless and at our worst, Christ died for us (Romans 5:6:18).

God's love for us is unconditional. He is our Father, and we are his children.

He will do anything to save his children.

Jesus came to save us, not to condemn us through the law.

The law was good; the law was and still is right even today (Hebrews 10:1), but it was just a shadow of the good things to come. Jesus proved his love on the cross and fulfilled the scriptures, which said, "No sin should enter heaven."

Humanity could not live by the law. In Old Testament times, priests had to continually beg forgiveness for the sin of the people (Hebrews 10:1–8). In the Old Testament, the blood of animals was just a covering for sin, not salvation. God never desired the shedding of animals' blood, but he accepted it. Jesus died on the cross to take our sin away by shedding his blood as the lamb. His last words were, "It's finished."

Jesus came to save us while we were at our worst—when we had that pipe, that bottle, that needle, and so on. He unconditionally asks us to come back home.

- There is nothing you've done and nothing you can do to earn God's love because you already have it.

Faith

Faith is the substance of things hoped for but not yet seen.

We are not saved by faith and works but by faith that works.

Patience

Secret: Remember that God is more interested in changing you than in changing your circumstances.

Patience leads to perfection. An old song is titled "Jesus Will Fix It after a While."

- Stay on the potter's wheel so you don't end up in the potter's field.

Patience brings perfection. Jesus was made perfect through the things he suffered: "God has made everything beautiful in its own time" (Romans 8:18–19).

This is my mother's favorite song.

You can't, hurry God, you just got to wait. You got to trust him, and give him time.

No matter how long it may take.

He's a God, you can't hurry. He'll be there, don't you worry.

He may not come when you want him, but he's right on time.

Right on time. Right on time.

Secret: Think about the end before you begin to seek something. Don't rush into something if you haven't fully considered the outcome.

- "It's not the years in life that count; it's the life in those years that counts" (Abraham Lincoln).

Secret: If you wish to accomplish anything, you must first expect it of yourself.

Story

President Lincoln invited some of his friends over for a discussion. They sat at a conference table drinking coffee from cups and saucers. Lincoln noticed that some were frowning and cutting their eyes at an old country fellow who was pouring his coffee from his cup into his saucer and sipping his coffee from the saucer. He started drinking his coffee that way as well. All eyes were focused on Lincoln. One after the other began to do the same. Everyone smiled as they admired how the president had saved the old country fellow from embarrassment and had saved them from themselves.

Secret: The greatest way to lead is by example.

2

CHAPTER

How Many Fish Can You Clean before You Catch Them?

How to Respond to Those Expressing Dysfunctional Behavior

This chapter is a must for parents, teachers, caregivers, counselors, and others who deal with people struggling with dysfunctional behavior.

On the following page, you will find a valuable diagram entitled High Love/Low Love. It's easy to understand, and it will help you help those in your care. It explains how and why those in your care can be submissive, spoiled, rebellious, and apathetic.

Outside the circle is the individual applying the treatment. Inside the circle is the individual being treated. The arrow pointing from the inside circle to the oval shape is the projected results of the treatment.

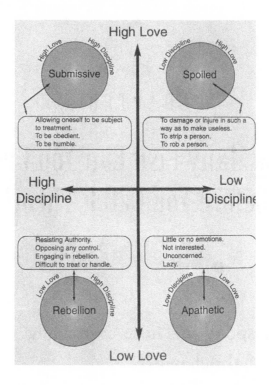

For those who are overtaken in misconduct.
You are to restore him in a Spirit of Gentleness.
(Galatians 6:1)

Secret: God knows who we are. God knows where we have been. God knows what we have been though. He knows why we are the way that we are. And God works with each one of us accordingly. (Romans 9:20–21)

Someone with an eating disorder has no right to condemn the drug addict and vice versa. We all have issues we have not yet conquered.

Don't get discouraged while responding to love ones or other concerned individuals in your care while they are struggling with behaviors.

Remember, only God can change a person. You can't even change you. God does the changing.

God told Moses to stretch his hand out across the Red Sea. Moses couldn't stretch his hand across the Red Sea, but God could.

Secret: Those who struggle with their strongholds must be ready to change and search for change as though they were searching for silver and gold. If they cannot do that, they are not ready to change.

Secret: One of the first signs of recovery is truthfulness.

Secret: Denial is part of the addiction.

Before the will of God can be done, it has to be known.

Secret: You must first win over others trust before you can try to correct their faults. Otherwise, they will see you as preaching to them, being negative, or putting them down (Hebrews 5:11–14).

- Beginners need milk, not solid food.

Secret: You can't solve the problem by condemning the person. Condemn the problem, not the person.

- You might think that if someone else doesn't change, you won't be happy. That's codependency.

You are codependent when your happiness depends on whether your loved one is happy or not; it's called the methadone effect. Methadone is a medication given to heroin addicts that gives them everything they get from heroin except the high. Whenever addicts get high and abuse their financial resources, anxiety, depression, and unhappiness follow, and the codependent (you) also feels anxious, depressed, and unhappy. The codependent gets everything the addict gets except the high.

God never intended for you to carry the burdens of those who aren't ready to receive guidance. It is hard for us to give in and give it to God. Our ways are not like God's ways.

Secret: At some point, we need to know when to stop playing God. Only God can do the changing. In many cases, God is not done with that person yet.

After Jesus rose from the dead, he gathered his disciples and explained to them that they could do even greater works than he had done. He told them to go out and preach the Word. He said that wherever they were not received, they were to shake the dust off their feet and leave.

Story

An old fellow sitting on his porch noticed something wobbling on a branch of his tree. He got up for a closer look and saw that it was a cocoon. He thought, *A caterpillar trying to become a butterfly. Let me help it out.* He pulled out a pocketknife and carefully zipped the cocoon open. There it was—half-caterpillar and half-butterfly. It died. God was not done with it yet. God knows the why, when, and how.

Secret: You never know God till you know darkness.

Getting through trials, tribulations, and adversities perfects us. We sometimes want the resurrection without the Gethsemane, in which Jesus endured pain and agony.

We sometimes want the "mony" without the "test," the testimony.

- Sometimes God allows for pain as a deterrent.
- Pain helps us to consider the consequences.

Secret: Sometimes in the event of trying to rescue others, we interfere with God's plans. Many times, God is not done with them yet.

- Stop trying to do God's work. You can't change anyone.

Start trusting God for everything. You have to have faith that God can do what he says he can do.

Walk by faith, not by sight.
When you walk by faith, you walk in the Spirit.
When you walk by sight, you walk in the flesh.
When you walk by faith, you are in for a fight.
God said, "Fight the good fight of faith."

Secret: As long as flesh and works are in place, you are trying to earn it per your performance, but that means you are operating under the law.

True Story

I wrote a letter to someone I was counseling. In it, I told her that if she kept doing this and that, this and that would happen because this equals that.

Then the Holy Spirit came to me and said, *You're speaking under the law. The law says two plus two equals four. You get what you deserve. You take a life, and your life may be taken.*

I discarded that letter and wrote her a letter of encouragement, a letter of grace and mercy. I told her that God would bring her out just as he had brought me out. I told her to have faith and keep up the good fight.

When something is bigger than you, give it to God.

When Jesus went to the cross, his blood subtracted sin from us. The law was and still is good and right, but God knew we wouldn't live up to the law. Jesus's death on the cross brought us from under the law and into grace.

Grace is stronger than sin. Grace is bigger than sin. Grace subtracts sin (Romans 8:1–5, 7:4–7, 10:1–5).

- The entire Bible points to the book of Romans.
- The Old Testament tells us that no sin will enter heaven. Jesus came—purchased us from the Old Testament—and brought us into grace so the scripture would be fulfilled (Romans 8:4).

God's ways sometimes don't make sense to us because God made all the sense.

Let's take that burden off our shoulders and stop worrying and pulling out our hair over those who struggle with their behavior.

- Preaching to them, being negative, or condemning them will only drive them away.

Secret: *You can be right all the time and still be alone.*

You can love them, but God does the changing. (Romans 14:4; John 14:1–6). Jesus explained to his disciples that he was going away to prepare a place for them—heaven—and there they would be also.

- Thomas said to Jesus, "Lord, no one have showed us the way to Heaven." Jesus said, "I am the Way, the Truth, and the Life."

A problem is a problem is a problem.

We all have issues. Some issues will spiral you downward faster than others.

Those who suffer from eating disorders, drug abuse, or alcohol, struggle just as much as do those who suffer from addictions to pornography and other traps.

We all are fighting for our lives against our issues. We try not to think of our problems; we fight to keep them off our minds, but too often, they overtake us and off we go as if we were being seduced by sirens. Drugs, gambling, porn, or adultery overtakes our flesh as they have done so many times before. For many of us, it seems like for a lifetime.

Remember that change is the most difficult thing for us to accomplish. We have to recognize, organize, prioritize, and energize ourselves if we want to change; we have to seek change as if we were searching for silver and gold.

Note: You basically have to plea to God for change because you can't change yourself; only God can. We have been hurt, depressed, and unhappy. We are anxious and lack confidence. God help us. We are getting tired of that short-term pleasure resulting in long-term pain.

When will I awake so I can find another drink? (Proverbs 23:35)

Time will dare those who suffer from addictions to adultery, eating disorders, gambling, and so on. Never think you are better than a drug addict or an alcoholic because we all have issues. The adulterer suffers as much as the crack addict or the gambler does. If not for God, we would all go down, and some issues will take us down sooner than others.

What difference does it make if we all end up in the same place? Is it okay to brag that I arrived in hell or heaven sooner than you did? If we don't seek change, we all may very well end up in the wrong place.

It is not always the swift who wins the race.

It's not how you start; it's how you finish.

Let's stop being so critical of others; they may not have the same issues that we do. Many times, I've heard crack addicts say, "At least I don't do heroin!" They are unaware that they may be inviting God to judge them as they have judged others.

Secret: When you are focusing on others, you are neglecting yourself. As the old folks say, "The pot can't talk about the kettle." We all have issues.

- Have you mastered your issues, or have your issues mastered you?

Secret: You can walk away from whatever you have mastered, but you cannot walk away from whatever you have not mastered.

Secret: When you condemn someone else, you are condemning one of God's children. It won't be long before you start condemning the one who created that child—God.

Secret: You can judge a tree by its fruit, but you wouldn't be so quick to judge the tree if you knew its roots.

True Story

During my early years growing up in the South, we had no running water in our house. Naomi, my older sister, had planted fig trees on both sides of our porch at the same time, but one flourished and bore plenty of figs while the other barely grew and produced only a fig or two.

When my siblings and I would get mad at each other, we'd say, "You're as worthless as that little fig tree, a waste of time!"

Dad was generally a quiet man, but when he had enough of us arguing, he would speak with knowledge and wisdom and would get our attention. He'd say, "Do you know why that little fig tree doesn't grow? It's because when you empty the pan of water you've washed the dishes in, you toss it on the little fig tree, and the food crumbs attract insects that eat its leaves. That's why the little fig tree can't grow. Stop all your fussing."

If you knew the history, the roots, you wouldn't be so quick to judge.

What do you desire?

Shall I come to you with a rod or with love? (1 Corinthians 4:20–21).

Secret: Your character can promote or prevent your victory.

What seeds are you planting? Good seeds? Bad seeds? They can produce a hundredfold, perhaps a thousand fold of good fruit or bad fruit.

True Story

One time when I was in the day room with the teen boys at an outreach, several of them started running through the home. I pleaded with them to stop the running. I verbally attacked one of them, and he struck back at me with profanity. I said, "God is going to get you, boy. You're going to get it!" Just then, the Holy Spirit told me, *Wait a minute. There is a reason these children are this way.*

The Holy Spirit reminded me of the time I was in a crack house waiting to be served. I saw two children crawling on the floor as other adults smoked and drank as they sat on couches. I thought, *Man, these children's lives are going to be messed up.*

At the outreach, the Holy Spirit told me, Can't you see? *Remember? These are the little children whose lives you said were going to be messed up.*

Wow! A light turned on in my head. I realized I knew the teens' history. That's why you shouldn't judge others until you know their history. That was a life-changer for me. You can't hurt someone else without hurting yourself.

Be careful you who condemn others but then go looking for your next drink.

3

CHAPTER

There Is Always a High Price to Pay for Low Living

Secret: No matter what your past may have been, your future is spotless.

This chapter will help you recognize the devil's deceitful tricks and schemes.

- Until you see your difficulties as mountains, you will not succeed.

God gives you a choice. He stood right by and allowed Satan to use Adam. But he will protect your rights even unto eternal death. Start speaking the Word, not the problem (Joshua 1:8).

- Confession precedes possession. Start confessing the Word over your children and loved ones as well as over yourself.

Secret: When you speak and confess the powerful Word of God, you allow God to bring it to pass, and your faith will increase when you see God's mighty hand at work.

- It works because God created all the works.

When you expect something, be at your best in preparation to receive it.

- It's not so much up to God how prosperous you become; it's how you live.

Ignorance is the breeding ground of bondage (Hosea 4:6).

- Seek the Lord while he may yet be found. Otherwise, you may end up in a pit.

Secret: Don't get comfortable in a pit. A pit is anywhere you don't want to be, and cannot get out of it on your own.

A pit can be a form of bondage. There are many ways you can end up in a pit. You can be led into one. Someone can toss you into a pit. You can ignore the warning signs—Stop. Yield. Turn Back. Detour. Slippery Slope Ahead.

However you end up in a pit, God can use it for your good. Remember Joseph and Jeremiah, who were tossed into pits.

Secret: Sometimes, the reason you can't get the victory can be traced back to your character and the way you treat others.

When you are focusing on others, you are neglecting yourself.

When things are bigger than you, stop and give it all to God. Where you can't, he can,

Note: Never say to God, "Okay, I got this situation from here on out." God may say, "Okay, I'll get out of your way and let you fix it."

- Can anyone outsmart God?
- You might get your way and win the battle of war rather than the battle of life.
- The battle belongs to the Lord.
- You can't worry or grieve yourself to victory.
- If you are not determined to seek God, you will be left wanting.
- Some seek God's hand and not his face.
- Give God praise before you tell him your problem.

Even if you don't see anything happening, something is happening. If the walls don't fall down the first time, keep marching. Rise, step forward, and possess the land.

This Christian walk is a walk more about faith than reality. God is looking for faith and obedience. He did not intend for us to march around and around the walls. God looks for our obedience through faith.

Secret: If you see only with your eyes, you won't see. If you gaze at the Bible more than you pray, be careful.

Do you have a true relationship with God? How often do you talk with him?

- Jesus said, "He who comes to me, under no circumstances will I turn him away."
- Every disease is curable, but not every patient is.
- God takes no pleasure in destroying (Ezekiel 33:11).
- He who calls upon the name of the Lord shall be saved.
- One of the sad parts of life is when you hear somebody talking about what could have been (Joshua 6:13).
- "Thinking is such a difficult thing. That's why so many don't do it" (Abraham Lincoln).

Boys, girls, men, and women, be careful not to participate in situations known to be wrong or the devil's work.

You can't hurt someone else without hurting yourself.

Secret: Your greatest enemy is yourself. Know thyself. Satan knows you. Satan is trying to destroy you, so know yourself.

It may be hard at times of trials, tribulations, and adversities to rest in God's love and accept his promise of protection, but we should always. He knows what is best for those he has promised to bless. God is his own interpreter and is able to make everything plain.

A promise can be of no account if you have no confidence in the promisor, but God is not a man; he does not lie.

- The Bible tells us that the Word of the Lord is true (Psalm 18:20).
- The Word is true from the beginning (Psalm 119:160).
- He cannot deny himself (2 Timothy 2:13).
- The Lord is not slack concerning his promises (2 Peter 3:9).
- He remembers his holy promises (Psalm 105:42).
- There is only one thing our loving God ever forgets— the sins of the believers.
- Their sins and iniquities will I remember no more (Hebrews 10:17).

Secret: Never be afraid of the devil, but be prepared for him.

Secret: God is not preparing the blessing for you; he is preparing you for the blessing.

- Whenever you see Satan at work, it is always about division.

When you get involved in immoral behavior, you are defiling God's temple. You are not your own; you were brought at a price—Jesus's death and resurrection.

The best way to make a difference in someone else's life is to make a difference in yours. You can't do that, but God can.

- God does the changing.
- There is no good in the flesh.
- You can't change you; only God can.

The Bible says put up the good fight of faith. God increases your faith to the degree you desire it.

"The battle is the Lord's," says the Lord.

"Don't be wise in your own eyes," says the Lord.

In 1 Samuel 3:4–14, we read that Eli let his children go without restraint; he had two hoodlum sons, and he did not stand for anything. He allowed anything in his house except the Lord.

Without vision, people perish.

Secret: If you don't stand for something, you will fall for anything.

True Story

I was assigned a preacher in a rehab house. He pulled me to the side and spoke the most eye-opening words during my road to recovery: "Your problem is a pride problem. Not the kind of pride that makes you think you're better than others or that makes you walk in such a majestic manner thinking you are Mr. It. You have the worst kind of pride—pride of self. You put yourself ahead of mother, father, sister, brother, wife, children, and most of all, God. Think! All that money you have spent on your addiction— who was that for? It was for you! You could have given it to your children, the church, charities, or the needy, but no, it was all for you. You put yourself before everyone else."

My friend, the devil is very tricky. I bet if you looked at yourself, the devil would say, "Look at you. You need to start doing something for yourself," but what he won't tell you is that what you have been doing all the time was for yourself.

I know this does not make you feel good; it's supposed to hurt to the point that you don't want to ever get yourself in that shape again.

Secret: Sometimes, what might seem like your darkest moment can very well be your finest hour.

- Again, you never know God till you know darkness.
- Again, the devil will tell you everything except how you are going to end up.

One of the greatest gifts God gave man is freedom of choice, one of God's highest principles.

Once appointed a time in Heaven.

God Spoke to Lucifer. I created you perfectly, full of wisdom and beauty. Because of your beauty, you corrupted your wisdom. Now, Lucifer, you have said in your heart that you would exalt your throne above my stars.

Lucifer: I want to be like you, God, the Most High! In fact, I want to be greater than you. I want all the angels here in heaven to follow me. You gave us a choice. Look at my beauty. You made me a highly exalted angel, a leader. I am breathtaking! A third of your angels now follow me.

God: Because of your pride and jealously, you are trying to destroy my followers to bring pain and sorrow. I created angels that they may be happy, joyful, and peaceful as they worship me. There shall be no other God before me.

A war broke out in Heaven

God: There is no place in heaven for you and the angels that follow you. I will cut you down! I saw you fall from heaven like lightning.

Now, this world (Earth) is Satan's new headquarters.

God sat aside a place on earth called Eden. God placed a garden in Eden for mankind. God handcrafted man with his very own hand. God gave man dominion over the earth.

Satan: That law you gage man. He couldn't even keep that one and only law! You put him in that beautiful garden, and I deceived him. He listened to me and ate from the tree. Now, I have brought separation between you and that man you crafted.

God: That law I gave man was just a shadow of good things to come. I have taken away the first to establish the second, and what the law could not do, I will send my Son to do.

Satan: You crafted me as a perfect and sinless angel. You gave me a choice. You knew I would rebel from the beginning. I know my time is short. You knew from the beginning that I would go after the woman to stop the birth of your Son. I am not done yet!

God: For this purpose, my Son was manifest that he might destroy all your works.

One day on earth, God's angels came to present themselves before the Lord. Satan also came with them to present himself before the Lord.

God: Satan, where have you come from?
Satan: The earth. I am going back and forth there.
God: Have you considered my servant Job?
Satan: Take that hedge from around him and we will see.

God: I give you all the power to do what you want except don't take Job's life.

Satan hated God and all his followers; he would do anything in his power to bring pain and sorrow to God and his people. Satan has a good track record of bringing affliction to God's children. Satan remembered how he had brought death to man in the garden. He had not forgotten how he had brought so much discouragement to God in the day of Noah that God repented that he had made man (Genesis 6:6). Only Noah and his family followed God; the rest of the people on earth perished in the flood.

Satan broke God's heart again as God brought the Hebrews out of bondage in Egypt, but only two original people made it into God's Promised Land.

Although Satan failed to take Job's life, Satan realized that almost the entire world followed him because of his lies.

Satan: I am not done yet! Before Jesus comes the second time, I will appear as an angelic being posing as Christ. Your only hope is not to listen to me (Matthew 24:23–26).

God: Depart from me, you cursed being, into the everlasting fire prepared for you and your demons (Matthew 25:41). Because you brought death into this world, I have used the death of my Son to destroy you, Satan, once and for all! (Hebrews 2:14).

Trouble will not rise up a second time (Nahum 1:9; Ezekiel 28:1–26; Luke 10:18; Isaiah 14:13–14; Revelation 12:1–13).

Warning: when we lie, misquote others, run others reputations into the ground, cause conflict, slander anyone, or do any other work of the devil, that can be traced back to our failures in life.

Good News Report

No matter how stained your past is, your future is spotless.

Whom will you serve—the creature or the Creator?

When you do the devil's work, you will feel ugly inside, and that will cause you to search outside yourself, and that can lead to addictions of all sorts.

- When you have peace, that represents the presence of the Lord.

4

CHAPTER

Confession

Secret: If you have a question, call the Lord. His number is Jeremiah 33:3: "Call unto me, and I will show thee great things, and I will answer thee and show thee difficult things which thou know not."

Secret: Sometimes, things that can heal you are the hardest to do.

Secret: Some problems can never be solved until you confess them to one another.

- He who covers his sins shall not prosper, but he who confesses his sins shall obtain mercy (Proverbs 28:13).
- Denial is darkness. Confession is light; choosing between them means choosing between eternal life and eternal death.
- Confession means, "Yes, I did that, but I can and will do better."
- As long as you justify what you do, you won't feel a need to confess what you have done.

Confession is for you. It frees you from having to hide, duck, deceive, and lie. It's good for the soul. When you confess to others, it allows them to be encouraged that they too can be changed.

- We all need repentance.
- "In repentance and rest, you shall be saved. In quietness and trust he would be your strength" (Isaiah 30:15).

Note: Repent first. God never wanted us to worry about the things of this world. Confess it and put it in God's hands. This relieves you of carrying the load of stress, anxiety, and depression. God wants for you to stop trying to figure it out and give it to him.

- Look at life like a wheel; what you put on it will keep coming around and around.

- God never wanted us to carry the unnecessary load of anxiety, worry, depression, and lack of confidence. The Bible says worrying is a sin. If it goes on for too long, our God-given joy, peace, and happiness will be overtaken by sorrow and ugliness. Soon, our inner person will be searching for joy, peace, and happiness outside of self in the form of addictions of all types.
- Before you possess anything, you must first confess it. You have what you say that you have.
- Those who conceal their sin shall not prosper, but those who confess their sin shall obtain mercy (Proverbs 28:13).

Secret: Surrender. Only in the Christian world can the word *surrender* refer to power, prestige, and gain.

- When we lift our hands in praise to God, we are saying, "I surrender. I give up. I won't try anything. You got me" just like in Westerns. Christians lift their hands to the Lord to acknowledge there is no one greater than him. They are saying, "Thank you, Lord, for saving little me."
- When we bow our heads during praise and worship, we are saying, "God, you are the Most High, and little me is not worthy of looking up at your majesty."

This is how our attitude should be with God—"Lord, I give up. I surrender. My life is in your hands."

God will come to save the broken.

Secret: Remember that sometimes, the hardest thing to do is the thing that can heal you. We would love to have the healing, but in many cases, the price is too high.

Story

A woman doing some window-shopping saw a beautiful dress on a mannequin and thought, *Wow! I'd love to have that dress! This would look beautiful on me.* She got closer and spotted the price tag. *Too much for me*, she thought. Her admiration for the dress hadn't changed, but she considered the price too high.

Your walk with God is a faith walk. When you want more from God, you have to bring him more. It's hard to trust what you don't see.

Jesus said that we were his friends and that he has made known to us everything he learned from the Father. The Bible said that Jesus was made perfect by the things he endured.

- Everything comes with a price. You are who your character is.
- A man without good character becomes a real character.
- True repentance means that you are sorry for what you have done and that you intend not to do it again.

You might do it again, but you definitely intend not to.

- Life is not about the moment; life is about the movement. Give him milk before meat.

God is in the business of forgiveness. Repentance means you have had a change of heart.

Every decision you make affects someone else—your children, your loved ones, and others as well as yourself.

- What we do affects others.
- Light equals confession (1 Peter 2:9).
- The goodness of the Lord is design to get you to repent.
- When you consider the goodness of God, you will repent.

The lack of repentance causes the load you carry to become too heavy. God wants you to give it to him and let it go; he will carry it.

- Repentance is like forgiveness. You will be forgiven to the degree that you understand forgiveness.

Story

An old man was carrying a sack of potatoes when another man and his son passed him on the road. The man said, "Hey, old fella, we're going to town too. We'll give you a ride there."

The old fellow said, "No, I don't want to bother nobody."

"But my son and I don't want you to carry such a heavy load."

The old fellow finally agreed to ride with them. He got on the wagon with the sack still on his shoulder. "Why are you still carrying that heavy sack?" the man asked,

The old fellow replied, "Like I said, I don't want to bother nobody."

- Sometimes, it's hard for us to let go and let God.

In this life, we are preparing for the life to come.

- We argue with God because we have areas of independence and don't want to let go.

Secret: Do you want to stop sinning? Grace stops sin (Titus 2:11–12). You can't, but God can and did stop the sin on the cross through grace. You can't earn grace. You don't deserve grace. Regardless of what you do, it won't be enough to earn grace. One step at a time, you will get better little by little as you mature. You first drink milk, and later, you eat meat until the day of Jesus Christ.

Secret: Before you can discover who you are, you have to discover who you are not.

- We have everything to produce the fruit of holiness in us. Everything produces after its own nature, and we have a new nature called grace.
- Every blessing is a result of grace.
- Give up your rights for the sake of your brothers and sisters. Yes, you may have been mistreated and offended, but let it go. That's grace in action.
- You are the resource, which comes after the source—God.
- Jesus is here to break your spirit of addiction.
- Confession is light while denial is darkness.

God wants you to stop trying to figure it out because you can't all by yourself. There is no scripture, song, psalm, or sermon that will open your eyes and change you overnight.

- It's through repentance and rest that you will be saved.
- It's by the movement, not by the moment, from the Old Testament to the New Testament, from Egypt to the Promised Land, from Joseph coming out of a pit to becoming prince of Egypt.

5

CHAPTER

Gates to the Soul

Humanity has explored the skies, stars, planets, and the highest mountains. Humanity has surveyed the waters and measured the depths of the oceans, but humanity itself is God's greatest creation.

- God handcrafted us.
- He made us magnificent—just a little lower than the angels.
- He gave us unique gifts with which we communicate—tongues, ears, and eyes.

Secret: These God-given gifts are sometimes called gates to your soul. These gifts are thought containers. Seeds are planted and stored on the tongue and in the eyes and ears. These thought containers are seed containers.

- If you don't know the purpose of something, you will always misuse and abuse it.
- Good news: Jesus said that we were his friends and that he has made known to us everything he learned from the Father.
- Jesus said that God's mysteries are gifts he is passing to us.

Secret: Everywhere you go, carry kindness with you.

- your tongue
- your eyes
- your ears
- through grace

What we say, see, and hear should be used as tools as to encourage, direct, and uplift others and ourselves.

- Salt is a preservative that retards spoilage; so should our communication be (Colossians 4:6).
- A word is a silent thought. Make sure it does not harm others.
- We are blessed when we can give a friendly word and friendly answer; the most safe and friendly response

is yea or nay; the Bible says let your speech be yes or no.

- Let your speech always seasoned with grace so you will know how to respond to others.

Through our speech, we can conduct ourselves with others in wisdom. Others can be quite different from us. Try to make others feel welcome in your presence.

Our prayer should be this.

Lord, have mercy on those who don't have. Those who are hungry. Those who are lost and can't find their way. Thank you, Lord, for helping those who are assisting those who are less fortunate. In your Son Jesus's name, amen.

- You can't save anyone. You can't even save yourself.

Secret: Other people's lives are changed by your testimony.

The devil is a trickster and a liar. He doesn't want you to tell your testimony of how you were once lost but are now found. If God found you, he can find others.

- Words have power. Words are thought containers.
- Words are seeds; they are types of Christ. They die, resurrect, are lifted up, and produce fruit.
- Words are important. By your words, you will be justified.
- A seed is the birth, life, death, and resurrection of Christ.

- There is no good in the flesh. When you die, others live. When Jesus died, I won.
- If you refuse to die to yourself, you will have some tough days ahead. The flesh has to die.

We are all pregnant with possibilities. Jesus said, "You see that grain of wheat? As long as you hold onto it, it will be only one grain, but as soon as you let go, drop it, cover it, and let die, it won't be long before it grows a hundredfold, a thousand fold."

Secret: Anything you don't feed will die.

Secret: If it eats, it's alive.

Secret: The same spirit that raised Jesus from the dead lives in you.

Secret: Do you know that your tongue is a type of seed?

- Life and death are in the power of your tongue.
- Words justify and condemn (Matthew 12:34–37).
- Where words are many, sin is not absent.
- No wonder Jesus said, "Let our words be yea or nay." Any other words can be costly.
- It is hard to take a thought into captivity when it comes from the mind and straight out of the mouth. That is not thinking; it is inconsiderate, bragging.

- The average man speaks twenty thousand words a day. The average woman speaks thirty thousand words a day.
- The tongue is like a double-edged sword; it cuts both ways.

The tongue is like a ship's rudder—one of the smallest but one of the most important parts of a ship; it can guide it to safety or steer it to destruction.

- If you are looking for a friend, be friendly.
- Words glorify the condition of our hearts.

My mother used to sing "Keep Your Mind Set on Jesus." Her last request to her children was, "Do everything without complaining or arguing" (Philippians 2:14).

We should imitate God because we are his dearly loved children. We should live lives of love just as Christ did; he gave himself up for us as a fragrant offering and sacrifice to God.

You were once darkness, but now, you are light in the Lord. The fruit of light consists of goodness, righteousness, and truth.

Find out what pleases the Lord. Have nothing to do with the fruit of darkness. It is shameful to be disobedient and do things in secret.

God's light makes everything visible. Wake up, sleeper. Rise from the dead, and Christ will shine on you.

• Have you developed an appetite for God?

God has given us a spirit so we can experience joy, peace, and happiness rather than anxiety, depression, sorrow, unhappiness, and a lack of confidence.

Be very careful, then, how you live—not as unwise but as wise. Make the most of every opportunity (Ephesians 5).

• Your old man has no place in your new life (Romans 6:6).

The book of Genesis tells us that before God created anything, he searched out its end to see if it was good. God then went back to the beginning and created it. Thinking from the end will save you time and many problems. Imitate Christ.

• Stop trying to figure it out. Only God can save you.
• Even our souls want to blame others for our problems.

The most dangerous member of our bodies including our arms, legs, hands, feet, and so on is the tongue. It is one of the smallest parts of us and weighs very little, but only a few men can hold their tongues.

True Story

One day when I was working with teens at an outreach, one boy and I were going back and forth in a heated argument. My son heard the commotion and came into the dayroom, where the young man and I were arguing. He said, "Dad, you're making things worse! Go to the office. I'll sit with the boys."

My feelings were hurt by the way my son had spoken to me. I was ashamed by the way I had conducted myself with that youth. I was wounded for the rest of the day, and I took that shame and anxiety home with me that evening.

The next day as I drove to work, I thought, *It was my fault for arguing with that boy. My words made him angry. I know I said them on purpose just to make him angry. Keep your big mouth closed today, and don't say words that cause problems.*

The Holy Spirit told me, *That's why you can't solve the problem. You're looking in the wrong place. You're blaming your tongue.*

The Holy Spirit let me know that my tongue was just the spokesperson for the rest of my body because my legs, arms, and so on could not speak. The Holy Spirit was saying, *Stop blaming your tongue. You have a heart problem. Out of the abundance of the heart, the tongue speaks.* The Holy Spirit revealed the truth—what I had said had come from my heart, and I had intentionally wounded that boy. Tears began to flow down my face. I was hurt and ashamed. I was exposed. The truth came out; the light came on—I was the problem.

Thank you, Lord, for showing me who I really am.

Secret: We are all responsible for ourselves.

Are you going to react to the offender, or are you going to respond to God's Word?

Secret: One of the greatest attributes anyone can possess is the desire to become a better person.

Secret: Life is not about the moment. Life is about the movement.

- God gives us milk before he graduates us to the meat of life.
- God speaks to us about the tongue, a double-edged sword that can cut both ways.
- The Bible tells us that the issues of life flow out of the heart. We all have issues—heart conditions.

Secret: You'll never solve the problem by blaming your tongue because the tongue speaks only what's in your heart.

- The Bible tells us not to trust the heart because it is deceitful.
- Oh Lord, who can save my soul from this wretched man I am?
- The Bible tells us that there is no good in the flesh.

Secret: Anything you feed the flesh turns to waste.

- No wonder the old hymn tells us, "Keep Your Eyes on Jesus."
- Our ways are not God's ways.
- The reason we can't solve our problems is that we are looking in the wrong places for the solutions.
- We blame our tongues, but we should blame our hearts.

Secret: The tongue speaks out of the abundance of the heart.

Secret: The flesh needs to be saved. The Holy Spirit, who dwells in us, can change us.

- The flesh wants to go to hell.
- We are naturally flesh; we try to be independent of God.
- Wake up, O sleeper—arise from the dead and Christ will shine on you.

God has given us some of his greatest gifts—our tongues, ears, and eyes.

If you don't know the purpose of something you will always abuse it.

1. The tongue: Noah's son saw his dad in the tent naked and told others about that. God cursed the son for telling. **You can't tell everything.**

2. The eye: David saw Bathsheba taking a bath. He had her husband killed so he could have her. **Be careful what you let your eyes see.**

3. The ear: Delilah pressed and pressed Samson for where his strength was. **She heard it and told the enemy, which led to Samson's death.**

Secret: The darkness of sin is pleasure. Sinners love darkness rather than light because their evil deeds are not exposed in darkness (John 3:19).

Note: Darkness is a place of ignorance; it is where God is not. Light can shine on our inner selves and shame us. We then seek joy, peace, and happiness outside ourselves but will never find it there.

- God created us in his likeness, but we lost that attribute after Adam and Eve's fall. Only God, our Creator, can restore our brokenness.

  Jesus is the image of God and the image of his person.

- Jesus is the image of the invisible God. When we see Jesus, we see the Father and what we should have been and where we should be—in an unbroken fellowship with God.

Christ came to restore and save the lost. To be restored, our prayer should be "Create in me a clean heart, O God, and renew a right spirit within me" (Psalm 51:10).

6

CHAPTER

Come Clean, Dirty

Secret: The best way to find yourself is to lose yourself in service to others. Trust God to do the rest.

Secret: Part of your coming clean is getting involved in something bigger than your negative behaviors.

Secret: You must have a plan. The devil is alive. He has a plan to kill, steal, and destroy you. Your problem will not fix itself.

Secret: Establishing your own righteousness can easily occur when you fail to assemble with others (Romans 10:2–4).

Secret: You can't manage what you do not measure. Is it sustainable?

- Sin is not just a black-or-white matter. Sin is design to destroy. Remember, every time you sin, you hurt God, yourself, and others.
- Satan blinds your mind. Sin blinds you.

Secret: Know that your sins will find you out in your children, on the job, or in the community sooner or later.

- Put on the whole armor of God that you might be able to stand firm against the schemes of the devil (Ephesians 6:11–13).

Secret: Your success is in the Lord.

Secret: The secret of the Lord is with those who fear him.

- Solomon, the wisest man ever, said, "Fear God."
- Remember your purpose on earth is to serve others.

Secret: What you make happen for others, God will make happen for you.

- You can't get a harvest from something you have not invested in.
- Whatever you succeed in can be traced to someone you have honored.

- Whatever is missing in your life that you don't value is not your top priority.
- If you fail in your life, it can sometimes be traced to someone you dishonored.
- Jesus came to save you from your sins.
- Every sin has the potential of hurting someone else.
- Every sin is a result of collaboration.
- Sin has three stages—fascination, form, and then fall.
- Four steps which lead to the fall:

  1. Pride
  2. A haughty spirit
  3. The fall
  4. Destruction

Secret: The flesh doesn't want to be saved. It wants to go to hell.

- We love darkness rather than light because light exposes our sin.
- The light of the righteous rejoices, but the light of the wicked shall be put out.
- Come Clean. *There is always a high price for low living.*
- Pride keeps us from grace.
- Pride is the original sin.

Pride brings about a character of deception, disobedience, covetousness, rejection, un-thankfulness, presumption, anxiety, anger, restlessness, self-centeredness, and other character defects. If these character defects are not corrected, pretty soon, you will begin to feel ugly inside and lack joy, peace, and happiness; you'll seek those outside and be trapped by addictions of all types. As I said before, short-term pleasure leads to long-term pain.

Secret: Grace stops sin.

Secret: Erase the first and last letter in the word *sin* and you have I, the root of sin.

- If you believe God is good and is with you, good things will happen to you.
- One of your greatest attributes is counting your many blessings (2 Kings 6:15–17; Philippians 4:17).
- As the song says, "What a Friend We Have in Jesus."

  Grace and mercy are bigger than sin.

- Can you give up your rights for your brother or sister? Yes, he or she may have offended you, but can you let that go? Grace stops the sin.
- God is the father of grace.

  Grace and mercy—God shows you these even though you don't deserve them.

- Blessed is the one who hears and observes (Luke 11:28).

  God said, "I have sent watchmen to watch over you, but you would not listen!"

- Can we outsmart God? God always catches us in our craftiness.

Warning: After one has learned and turned back, it is better that he had not known. It is like a dog turning back to his own vomit, or a hog going back to his mud after being cleaned up (2 Peter 2:20–22; Proverbs 26:11).

Warning: Once a man has received grace and mercy—what Jesus provided us on the cross—his soul is clean of all sin. Therefore, if he does not fill his new, clean soul with God's Word, the old demon spirit will come back and occupy that clean soul and dominate and corrupt that man causing him to become worse than before.

Matthew 12:43–45 says that when the unclean spirit goes out of a man, it passes through waterless places seeking rest and does not find it. Then it says,

- I will return to my house (your clean soul), which I came, and when it comes, it finds it unoccupied, swept and put in order. Then it goes and takes along with it seven other spirits more wicked than itself, and they go in and live there, and the last state of that man becomes worse than the first. That is the way it will also be with this evil generation.

Jesus said, "In this generation, while seeing, they do not see, and while hearing, they do not hear, and do not understand." Jesus said, "The heart of this people has become dull." He said, "Lest they should see with their eyes and hear with their ears and understand with their Heart, and turn again and he (Jesus) will heal them" (Matthew 13:10–17).

Secret: Jesus spoke all these things in parables to fulfill what was spoken through the prophets. Jesus said, "I will open my mouth in parables, I will utter things hidden since the creation of the world."

Why is change so difficult? The most difficult thing for us to do is change.

Secret: You have to want to change, understand it with your heart, and turn to Jesus for help. Jesus promised, "He who calls upon him. He will not turn you away."

In the day of Moses, God allowed a whole generation of people to die because of their unwillingness to change. In the days of Noah, God explained that man's wickedness had become so great and that every inclination of the thoughts of man was evil all the time.

- God was grieved that he had made man on the earth, and God's heart was filled with sorrow. He was so disappointed with man's wickedness that he destroyed mankind and everything else that lived on earth. But he also demonstrated his grace by allowing Noah and his family to survive and reproduce humankind.

As long as we are flesh, our hearts will be deceptive, tricky, and untrustworthy. Even after God showed grace to Noah and his family, Noah got drunk and brought shame and a curse on his family. Humans are deceitful.

Question

Can God trust you to bless you? Are you going to be a good steward of what God has entrusted you with?

- Your gorgeous home?
- Your beautiful car?
- Your God-fearing spouse?

Answer

God is more interested in changing you than your circumstances.

Good News

If you want to find your purpose in life, lose yourself in service to others.

Let's pray this prayer again.

Lord, allow me to see me the way I really am. Not the way I see me, Lord, but the way you see me—the way I really am.

Lord, I know I can't change me, but you can change me. I acknowledge that change is your work. Thank you, Lord! **Secret:** Good character requires these personal qualities.

- obedience
- reverence
- love
- forgiveness
- gratefulness
- faith
- meekness
- patience
- determination
- flexibility
- courage
- humility

Remember, one of the greatest attributes you can possess is the desire to become a better person.

And yes, you can. Yes, you can.

7

CHAPTER

God Is Trying to Reproduce Himself in You

Secret: God made man as a companion for himself. Man is God's greatest creation. He made woman because he knew man needed a companion. Peter was a favorite friend of Jesus. Jesus appreciated friendship. God made man for himself. We are his children.

- When you identify with something, you will go to the extent of looking like it (Luke 19:41–44).
- The more you look at something, the more you will begin to look like it.

Love, peace, joy, happiness, and confidence in him are what God wants for us because he created us in the image of his character.

Secret: We will not feel complete until we take on the character of God.

Sometime during the course of your life, God will allow for you to be in a position that he will show himself to you.

Moses was in the desert from ages forty to eighty. God knows when we are mature enough; he knows the length of time we need in the desert.

Jesus died not just to lead us but also to change us.

God's character consists of believing, behaving, belonging, and becoming what he wants of us.

Secret: Jesus was made perfect through the things he suffered.

- God's will for you is stronger than your will to do it. The secret is to surrender yourself to him.

Secret: Some people never know who God is because they don't trust him.

- The heart of God is to give. God has needs also; he wants us to come back to him. God gave his Son so that we could come back home to him.

- God asks of us; that shows he needs us.
- God's character is a promise: he can't lie or forget; he knows all and can do all. He can call anything into existence.

Secret: If you are the smartest person in your group, your group is too small.

An old African saying is "I am who I am because of you. You are who you are because I am."

Jesus learned obedience through the things he suffered (Hebrews 5:8).

You can't alter behavior until you alter your thoughts. As a man thinks, so he is.

Freedom is not the right to do what you want but the right to do what you should.

Secret: The quality of your decisions determines the quality of your life.

Jesus was not a people pleaser. Whenever he finished doing a great work for the father, he separated himself from the people.

Note: I wrote this book not for those who fit in but for those who stand out. Stop trying to fit in!

- The heart of man says that there has to be more to life than this. We are a desperate people wanting more and more.

The principle of navigation is the principle of the fixed laws of nature and creation.

In the old days, pioneers used the stars to calculate their position and to figure out where they were going.

A compass cannot move without the force of gravity, which God created.

Secret: The secret of success is submitting to the law of principles.

Secret: You want to be successful? Duplicate success!

Your decisions should be made to benefit where you want to go.

The key to feeling confident comes from the fact that you know principles.

Secret: Principles protect you from damaging facts.

- Principles are permanent.
- Principles are the key to navigation.
- Speak principles, not facts, even when you read the Bible.

Here are three questions you should ask yourself when you read the Bible:

1. What does it teach me about God?
2. What does it teach me about humanity?
3. What does it teach me about the devil?

- Before anything was, God was. When God made man, man was completely loaded. God put everybody in one body—Adam's. God does not begin something until he finishes it.

Secret: Strive to be like God. Think about the end before you begin, because you would not start certain things if you knew how they would end.

- Assume you are what you want to be.
- Stay in contact with the source; you are the resource.
- A principle should never be confused with an opinion.
- Nothing is free. There is even a cost for forgiveness—it's called consequences.
- Stay on the potter's wheel so you don't end up in the potter's field among the weeds and thorns.
- Can a man outsmart God? Can a man successfully establish his own ways?

Jesus said we were his friends. He came here to show us the way and unchanging principles and how to navigate life. He is here to show us how to have joy, peace, and happiness.

- God said that we could do nothing without him, and without him, that's exactly what we can do—nothing.

When we do things our own way, we lose out on the love, peace, joy, and happiness God put in us and we end up depressed and anxious and lacking confidence. That causes our souls to become ugly, and we start searching for joy, peace, and happiness outside of ourselves. That can lead us, as I said, to all kinds of addictions that offer short-term gain but long-term pain.

Secret: The sweetest fragrance is one that has been crushed.

- When God calls us, he calls us to die to ourselves and live for him.

Secret: The reason you can't stop sinning is that you are still alive to your flesh.

Secret: There is no place for your old man in your new life.

You don't make mistakes. You make choices.
—my granddaughter Jennessia

John L. Vinson SR. President and Founder
of (TORA) Teen Outreach Academy.

Following in the footsteps of my Father and Mother.
My Dad was a great Man. The ground work he laid in the
community as a leader can be measured among the best as
a Husband and Father.

During my six years journey of substance abuse. I was a
single parent. I couldn't stop the behavior on my own. I went
into a 13-month residential program. After I graduated. I
Started a 12-month Faith Base residential program called
(TORA) Teen Outreach Academy. I started this program
with the intent of helping others. I found that I was the one
which really got the help.

You can't help someone else without helping yourself.

In 1999 **Mr. Vinson was awarded by the Governor's Office.** In That same year. **TORA received nation attention** attached with a cash award from (CSAT) the Center for Substance Abuse Treatment out of Washington DC. Accompany with the award, **TORA was chosen to represent the state of Arizona as September being National Recovery Month.**

Picture of people raising flag is TORA's Logo. The people in this photo is my mother (The Old Lady) several of her grand-children, her foster children and friends.

The word TORA represent the First Five Books of the Old Testament. These books were written by Moses (Per God).

There are 34,805 Letters contained in TORA.

It is believed that all major events that has happen and will happen is hidden in code in these first five books of TORA.

Note: One of his sisters came up with the idea abbreviation for Teen Outreach Academy as TORA.

Following in the footsteps of those who came before him.

The best way to lead is by example.

I want my children and all of my Grand-children for generations to come, to always look up to my Dad John T. Vinson and My Mom Roxie Farr Vinson Price.

From me. John L. Vinson Sr. This book is the greatest gift. The best gift I have to offer to you. Love you more.

One of the greatest attribute that a person can posses is the desire to be a better person.

Roxie Farr Vinson Price
Sunrise
July 28, 1923
Sunset
August 16, 2018

My Mother's remains ware brought to the church funeral Services by way of Horse and Buggy.

When I was on drugs. Sometimes I would call my Mother on the phone in Texas. When she answered the phone. I couldn't say a word. I was usually depressed, no confidence and broken with sorrow from self-inflicted wounds. I would be hurt and full of tears. All I could say was Mama, Mama. Some-how she knew it was me on the phone. She would say "Baby, is that you?" She would Immediately start to pray on the phone. Wasn't long, Mom packed up and moved here to where her children lived. Mom said she is coming to help save her children. Mom left behind a 22 Acre Farm and a Half Brick Home. Soon after arriving here someone gave her a home. Mom started Saturday Sunday School. All children and family must attend! One member started preaching from those services and still over twenty years later is still preaching at one of the largest churches in the state. Mom did not lose a home or loose a child. Mom gained another home and helped save her sons off drugs. Today, her children are still drug free.

People from the church says my mom's children (Her Sons) Brought men able to hug other men without shame. Mom, like her Great Grand Pa. Joshua Farr. Inspired, Impacted and Empowered many.

It is not the years in life that count. It's the life in those years that count.

An old African proverb: I am who I am because of you. You are who you are because I am.

Great Grand Pa. Joshua Farr.

Born into slavery. Grand Pa. Joshua. Inspired, Impacted and Empowered everyone he seemed to have come in contacted with. His wife was so fair skinned that she was taken away from him till slavery was abolished. There was a street named after Grand Pa. Joshua called **The Old Joshua Farr Road** (Adjacent to Farm Road 2460 Bon Weir Texas. Grand Pa. Joshua Donated the First Acre of land to start what is **still known as the Biloxi Evergreen Cemetery.** One of his Grand Sons (Uncle Joe Farr) started a Burial Association (Life insurance) and Funeral Services to help properly bury the dead. Later the funeral services were handed over to what is now known as the Coleman's Mortuary. My Dad (John T. Vinson) was one of the **Burial Association** Secretary's.

Grand Pa. loved the Lord and passed down through the generations to Fear God.

When he spoke. Attention was given. Everyone listened. My Mom at 95 years old mentioned that she remembered seeing that old man with the beard (Grand Pa. Joshua) when she was about 7 years old.

The following picture is a photo of one of Grand Pa. Joshua's Children (Richard Farr SR.) and seated on bottom right hand side is (Richard Farr JR.) my mother's Dad alone with other sisters and brothers.

Still today. The fruit doesn't fall FARR from the tree.

Biloxi Cemetery working, November 26, 1951.

You can't hurt someone else without hurting yourself.

Notes

Notes

Notes

Notes

Notes

Notes

Notes

Notes

Notes

Notes

CPSIA information can be obtained
at www.ICGtesting.com
Printed in the USA
BVHW071504050819
555095BV00008B/1180/P